To Alan and Nora, upon whom so much depends —L.R.

For Rebecca, who loves things that grow and words that
(don't necessarily have to) rhyme —C.G

The author wishes to thank Teresa Marshall Hale, great-granddaughter of
Thaddeus Marshall Sr.; Rod Leith, Rutherford, N.J., borough historian; and the
Meadowlands Museum, Rutherford, N.J.

Visit us on the Web! rhcbooks.com
Educators and librarians, for a variety of teaching tools, visit us at RHTeachersLibrarians.com
Library of Congress Cataloging-in-Publication Data
Names: Rogers, Lisa Jean, author. | Groenink, Chuck, illustrator.
Title: 16 words: William Carlos Williams and "The red wheelbarrow" / by Lisa Rogers;
illustrated by Chuck Groenink.
Other titles: Sixteen words
Description: First edition. | New York: Schwartz & Wade Books, [2019] | Audience: 004-008.
Identifiers: LCCN 2018032228 (print) | LCCN 2018039482 (ebook) | ISBN 978-1-5247-2016-2 (trade)
ISBN 978-1-5247-2017-9 (lib. bdg.) | ISBN 978-1-5247-2018-6 (ebook)
Subjects: LCSH: Williams, William Carlos, 1883–1963—Juvenile literature. | Williams, William Carlos, 1883–1963.
Red wheelbarrow—Juvenile literature. | LCGFT: Picture books.
Classification: LCC PS3545.I544 (ebook) | LCC PS3545.I544 Z876 2019 (print) | DDC 811/.52—dc23
The text of this book is set in 13-point Deccan Medium.
The illustrations were rendered digitally.
MANUFACTURED IN CHINA
10 9 8 7 6 5 4 3 2 1
First Edition

16 Words

William Carlos Williams
& "The Red Wheelbarrow"

BY LISA ROGERS

ILLUSTRATIONS BY CHUCK GROENINK

schwartz & wade books · new york

Look out the window. What do you see?

If you are Dr. William Carlos Williams, you see—

A wheelbarrow. A drizzle of rain. Chickens scratching in the damp earth.

Perhaps Dr. Williams is waiting to read a thermometer. Maybe he has just written a prescription or, if his young patient feels up to a game, shuffled a deck of playing cards.

He looks up, looks out, and notices.

The wheelbarrow belongs to
Mr. Thaddeus Marshall. Dr. Williams
is the Marshalls' family doctor.

Day after day, Mr. Marshall picks up
his tools—a watering can, a rake, a trowel.
He cares for his garden at 11 Elm Street in
Rutherford, New Jersey.

Stepping around his chickens,

he turns the soil,

pulls weeds,

harvests greens.

He plucks ripe vegetables and carries
them to his wheelbarrow.
Then he lifts the wheelbarrow's
handles and balances it on its single tire.
His son Milton shoos the chickens away.

And Mr. Marshall pushes his wheelbarrow through the streets of Rutherford.

He depends on the wheelbarrow to carry the vegetables he sells to his neighbors.

Day after day, Dr. Williams also picks up his
tools—a stethoscope, syringes, a blood pressure
cuff, a thermometer, and more. He packs his
black doctor's bag and lifts it by its two handles.
He cares for patients in his office at 9 Ridge Road.
He cares for patients at their homes.

He bandages wounds,

checks temperatures, and listens to heartbeats.

He treats children with measles and chicken pox.

He brings many babies—at least
three thousand—into this world.

Dr. Williams depends on his doctor's bag to carry the tools he needs.

Along with his stethoscope and syringes, he carries a pen. A pen for writing prescriptions. A pen for crafting poems.

Writing poems brings Dr. Williams joy, and he fits in his writing around his doctoring.

If he's in his office, he uses the time between appointments to tap on his typewriter.

a fire engine,

He writes about trees,

cats,

and plums.

He chooses the words for his poetry as carefully as he examines his patients.

If he's making a house call, he scribbles
poems on his prescription pad.

He writes about his town and the people who live there.

Dr. Williams visits 11 Elm, where Mr. Marshall and his wife, Alice,
raised their sons, Milton, Hiram, Victor, Leon, and Thaddeus Jr.
Perhaps he is there to set a broken arm, or to soothe a high fever.
Perhaps he is caring for Mr. Marshall, who has been ill.

Dr. Williams pauses. He looks out the bedroom window toward the garden.

He sees rain falling.

It falls on the chickens scrabbling in the dirt, their feathers dingy white.

It falls on Mr. Marshall's wheelbarrow, red and weathered, sturdy and strong.

The rain streaks the window, soaks the garden, drips into the roots of Mr. Marshall's vegetable plants, helping them grow.

Dr. Williams grasps his pen. He begins
to write. He writes of what he notices—the
wheelbarrow, the chickens, the rain, the yard.
He writes a poem, using just sixteen words.

Those sixteen words do not describe
Mr. Marshall's chicken coop, or the train
rattling nearby.

They do not describe Mr. Marshall hefting
that wheelbarrow, or the aches and pains he
suffers from stooping to care for his plants.

They do not describe Mr. Marshall's life of
work or caring or love.

But somehow they say just that.

so much depends
upon

a red wheel
barrow

glazed with rain
water

beside the white
chickens

AUTHOR'S NOTE

Thaddeus Marshall (1852–1930) and his wheelbarrow inspired physician and Pulitzer Prize–winning poet William Carlos Williams's (1883–1963) most famous—and favorite—poem, "The Red Wheelbarrow," published in 1923.

Williams saw poetry in his patients' lives. He wrote of Marshall: "I liked that man, and his son Milton almost as much. . . . I suppose my affection for the old man somehow got into the writing."

As a young man, Williams had wanted to be an athlete, but he collapsed after a high school race and was found to have a heart condition. He was despondent. "Like a bolt out of the blue," his first poem came to him:

A black, black cloud
flew over the sun
driven by fierce flying
rain.

He felt such happiness that "from that moment I was a poet."

Williams created a new kind of poetry. Instead of formal rhymes and strict rhythmic patterns, his poems had unexpected line breaks, lacked capital letters, and left out punctuation. He used ordinary words and images.

When he ate plums that his wife was "probably saving for breakfast," he wrote the apology note "This Is Just to Say." After a fire engine zoomed by, he wrote "The Great Figure."

Williams's work with his patients also influenced his poetry. He felt he had to write down the "inarticulate poems" his patients' lives represented but that they could not write themselves.

We can't be sure what Williams felt when he wrote "The Red Wheelbarrow." When I learned about Marshall, I thought of how the two men respected each other. Was Williams making a connection between himself and the wheelbarrow's owner? That's what I believed, and what inspired me to write this story.

But Williams might not have meant that. "Sometimes when I write I don't want to say anything," he once said. "I just want to present it."

Just as someone can look and notice one thing, while someone else sees another thing, we all interpret poetry in our own way.

What does "The Red Wheelbarrow" mean to you?

SELECTED BIBLIOGRAPHY

Welshimer Wagner, Linda, ed. *Interviews with William Carlos Williams: "Speaking Straight Ahead."* New York: New Directions, 1976.

Williams, William Carlos. *The Autobiography of William Carlos Williams.* New York: Random House, 1951.

———. Edited by A. Walton Litz and Christopher MacGowan. *The Collected Poems of William Carlos Williams.* New York: New Directions, 1986.

———. Edited by Charles Tomlinson. *Selected Poems.* New York: New Directions, 1985.

———. "Seventy Years Deep." *Holiday* 16, no. 5 (November 1954): 78.

———. *Spring and All.* New York: New Directions, 2011.

SOME WILLIAM CARLOS WILLIAMS POEMS TO ENJOY

"The Great Figure"

"The Manoeuvre"

"Poem (as the cat)"

"This Is Just to Say"

"To"

"Winter Trees"